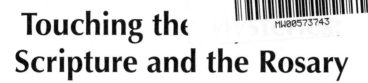

Touching the
Scripture and the Rosary

STUDY GUIDE

Catherine Upchurch

LITTLE ROCK SCRIPTURE STUDY

A ministry of the Diocese of Little Rock
in partnership with Liturgical Press

DIOCESE OF LITTLE ROCK

2500 North Tyler Street • P.O. Box 7239 • Little Rock, Arkansas 72217 • (501) 664-0340 • Fax (501) 664-6304

Office of the Bishop

Dear Friends in Christ,

The Bible comes to us as both a gift and an opportunity. It is a gift of God who loves us enough to communicate with us. The only way to enjoy the gift is to open and savor it. The Bible is also an opportunity to actually meet God who is present in the stories, teachings, people, and prayers that fill its pages.

I encourage you to open your Bibles in anticipation that God will do something good in your life. I encourage you to take advantage of the opportunity to meet God in prayer, study, and small-group discussion.

Little Rock Scripture Study offers materials that are simple to use, and a method that has been tested by time. The questions in this study guide will direct your study, help you to understand the passages you are reading, and challenge you to relate the Scriptures to your own life experiences.

Allow the Word of God to form you as a disciple of the Lord Jesus. Accept the challenge to be "transformed by the renewal of your mind" (Romans 12:2). Above all, receive God's Word as his gift, and act upon it.

Sincerely in Christ,

✝ J. Peter Sartain

✝ J. Peter Sartain
Bishop of Little Rock

Sacred Scripture

"The Church has always venerated the divine Scriptures just as she venerates the body of the Lord, since from the table of both the word of God and of the body of Christ she unceasingly receives and offers to the faithful the bread of life, especially in the sacred liturgy. She has always regarded the Scriptures together with sacred tradition as the supreme rule of faith, and will ever do so. For, inspired by God and committed once and for all to writing, they impart the word of God Himself without change, and make the voice of the Holy Spirit resound in the words of the prophets and apostles. Therefore, like the Christian religion itself, all the preaching of the Church must be nourished and ruled by sacred Scripture. For in the sacred books, the Father who is in heaven meets His children with great love and speaks with them; and the force and power in the word of God is so great that it remains the support and energy of the Church, the strength of faith for her sons, the food of the soul, the pure and perennial source of spiritual life."

Vatican II, Dogmatic Constitution on Divine Revelation, no. 21.

INTERPRETATION OF SACRED SCRIPTURE

"Since God speaks in sacred Scripture through men in human fashion, the interpreter of sacred Scripture, in order to see clearly what God wanted to communicate to us, should carefully investigate what meaning the sacred writers really intended, and what God wanted to manifest by means of their words.

"Those who search out the intention of the sacred writers must, among other things, have regard for 'literary forms.' For truth is proposed and expressed in a variety of ways, depending on whether a text is history of one kind or another, or whether its form is that of prophecy, poetry, or some other type of speech. The interpreter must investigate what meaning the sacred writer intended to express and actually expressed in particular circumstances as he used contemporary literary forms in accordance with the situation of his own time and culture. For the correct understanding of what the sacred author wanted to assert, due attention must be paid to the customary and characteristic styles of perceiving, speaking, and narrating which prevailed at the time of the sacred writer, and to the customs men normally followed in that period in their everyday dealings with one another."

Vatican II, Dogmatic Constitution on Divine Revelation, no. 12.

Instructions

MATERIALS FOR THE STUDY

This Study Guide: Touching the Mysteries: Scripture and the Rosary

Bible: The New American Bible with Revised New Testament or The New Jerusalem Bible is recommended. Paraphrased editions are discouraged as they offer little if any help when facing difficult textual questions. Choose a Bible you feel free to write in or underline.

Commentary: *Reflections on the Mysteries of the Rosary* by Mark G. Boyer (Liturgical Press) is used with this study. The assigned pages are found at the beginning of each lesson.

ADDITIONAL MATERIALS

Bible Dictionary: *The Dictionary of the Bible* by John L. McKenzie (Simon & Schuster) is highly recommended as a reference.

Notebook: A notebook may be used for lecture notes and your personal reflections.

WEEKLY LESSONS

YOUR DAILY PERSONAL STUDY

The first step is prayer. Open your heart and mind to God. Reading Scripture is an opportunity to listen to God who loves you. Pray that the same Holy Spirit who guided the formation of Scripture will inspire you to correctly understand what you read and empower you to make what you read a part of your life.

The next step is commitment. Daily spiritual food is as necessary as food for the body. This study is divided into daily units. Schedule a regular time and place for your study, as free from distractions as possible. Allow about twenty minutes a day. Make it a daily appointment with God.

As you begin each lesson read the assigned chapters of Scripture found at the beginning of each lesson, the footnotes in your Bible, and then the indicated pages of the commentary. This preparation will give you an overview of the entire lesson and help you to appreciate the context of individual passages.

As you reflect on Scripture, ask yourself these four questions:

1. *What does the Scripture passage say?*
   Read the passage slowly and reflectively. Use your imagination to picture the scene or enter into it.

2. *What does the Scripture passage mean?*
   Read the footnotes and the commentary to help you understand what the sacred writers intended and what God wanted to communicate by means of their words.

3. *What does the Scripture passage mean to me?*
   Meditate on the passage. God's Word is living and powerful. What is God saying to you today? How does the Scripture passage apply to your life today?

4. *What am I going to do about it?*
   Try to discover how God may be challenging you in this passage. An encounter with God contains a challenge to know God's will and follow it more closely in daily life.

THE QUESTIONS ASSIGNED FOR EACH DAY

Read the questions and references for each day. The questions are designed to help you listen to God's Word and to prepare you for the weekly small-group discussion.

Some of the questions can be answered briefly and objectively by referring to the Bible references and the commentary *(What does the passage say?)*. Some will lead you to a better understanding of how the Scriptures apply to the Church, sacraments, and society *(What does the passage mean?)*. Some questions will invite you to consider how God's Word challenges or supports you in your relationships with God and others *(What does the passage mean to me?)*. Finally, the questions will lead you to examine your actions in light of Scripture *(What am I going to do about it?)*.

Write your responses in this study guide or in a notebook to help you clarify and organize your thoughts and feelings.

THE WEEKLY SMALL-GROUP MEETING

The weekly small-group sharing is the heart of the Little Rock Scripture Study Program. Participants gather in small groups to share the results of praying, reading, and reflecting on Scripture and on the assigned questions. The goal of the discussion is for group members to be strengthened and nourished individually and as a community through sharing how God's Word speaks to them and affects their daily lives. The daily study questions will guide the discussion; it is not necessary to discuss all the questions.

All members share the responsibility of creating an atmosphere of loving support and trust in the group by respecting the opinions and experiences of others, and by affirming and encouraging one another. The simple shared prayer which begins and ends each small group meeting also helps create the open and trusting environment in which group members can share their faith deeply and grow in the study of God's Word.

A distinctive feature of this program is its emphasis on and trust in God's presence working in and through each member. Sharing responses to God's presence in the Word

and in others can bring about remarkable growth and trans-
formation.

THE WRAP-UP LECTURE

The lecture is designed to develop and clarify the themes of
the lesson. It is not intended to form the basis for the group
discussion. For this reason the lecture is always held at the
end of the meeting. If several small groups meet at one time,
the large group will gather together in a central location to
listen to the lecture.

Lectures may be given by a local speaker. They are also
available on audio- or video-cassette.

LESSON 1

Touching the Mysteries: Scripture and the Rosary
Reflecting on the Mysteries of the Rosary, **pages 7–19**

The Joyful Mysteries

Day 1

1. How would you describe your experience of praying the rosary?

2. In your prayer life, do you find it helpful to focus on events in the life of Jesus?

3. Is there one set of Mysteries (Joyful, Luminous, Sorrowful, Glorious) that appeals most to you? Why?

Day 2 The Annunciation

4. Read the two stories of the Annunciation of the birth of Jesus (Matt 1:18-25; Luke 1:26-38).

   a) Identify two or three major differences between the stories.

   b) Identify two or three similarities you find in the two versions.

5. What can we learn about divine "annunciations" from other biblical stories? (See Gen 18:1-15; Exod 3:4-14; Acts 9:10-19.)

6. What announcements have you experienced that help you appreciate the events surrounding the announcement of Jesus' birth?

Day 3 The Visitation

7. Try to imagine the meeting of the two pregnant women, Mary and Elizabeth (Luke 1:39-45).

   a) On a human level, what emotions would probably have surfaced between them?

   b) On a more symbolic level, what does their unity indicate about how God is acting on behalf of Israel? And about how God will act through their sons? (See Matt 3:3; 11:7-10; Luke 1:76-77.)

8. Elizabeth proclaims to Mary, "Most blessed are you among women, and blessed is the fruit of your womb" (Luke 1:42). Before being applied to Mary, for whom were such words used? (See Deut 28:4; Judg 5:24; Jdt 13:18.)

9. Compare Elizabeth's words to Mary in Luke 1:43 to those of King David in 2 Sam 6:9. What parallels can be gleaned from these passages?

Day 4 The Nativity

10. Read Matthew's version of the events surrounding the birth of Jesus (Matt 1:18–2:23). What are the indicators that Matthew is already helping his audience understand the mission of Jesus?

11. What details of Luke's version of the birth of Jesus (Luke 2:1-20) give us indications of his future mission?

12. In telling the story of Jesus' birth, what elements most affect you? Why?

Day 5 The Presentation at the Temple

13. Examine the account of Jesus being presented in the Temple (Luke 2:22-38). What can you learn from your Bible's foot-notes and cross references to help you understand the custom being described? (See Exod 13:2, 12; Lev 12:2-8.)

14. Simeon and Anna appear at the Temple as wisdom figures (Luke 2:25-38). What has prepared them to recognize Jesus for who he is?

15. Are there people in your life who help you to recognize God's action in your midst?

Day 6 Finding Jesus in the Temple

16. a) How did faithful Jews understand the role of the Temple? (See 1 Kgs 8:5-13; 2 Chron 6:14-21; Ps 27:4-5; 138:1-3.)

    b) Since Jesus' parents were faithful Jews, how do you think they felt finding their son in the Temple after three days of searching (Luke 2:41-52)?

17. Where did Jesus receive his apparent authority to question and respond to the elders (Luke 2:46-47)? (See Matt 7:28-29; Luke 4:36; 20:1-8.)

18. When has an experience of searching taught you something unexpected?

Suggestion: When praying these mysteries of the rosary, focus on the events in the life of Jesus and his parents, but also on the joy that each event represents for the church, for the world, and for you.

LESSON 2

Touching the Mysteries: Scripture and the Rosary
Reflecting on the Mysteries of the Rosary, pages 22–31

The Mysteries of Light

Day 1

1. Consider the properties of light. How do these properties prepare you to think about this newest set of mysteries of the rosary?

2. Jesus describes himself as "the light of the world" (John 8:12). How does this image help you understand Jesus and his public ministry?

Day 2 The Baptism of Jesus in the Jordan

3. The baptism of Jesus is recorded in all four gospel accounts (Matt 3:13-17; Mark 1:9-11; Luke 3:21-23; John 1:32-34). What are the common elements that you find in these accounts?

4. In what ways do the evangelists assure their listeners (and us) that although John baptized Jesus, it is Jesus who is the greater of the two? (See Matt 3:11-12; Mark 1:7-8; Luke 3:15-17; John 1:19-30.)

5. God calls Jesus "my beloved Son" (Matt 3:17; Mark 1:11; Luke 3:22). In your life, whose voices remind you that Jesus is God's Son, and that you are called to be like him?

Day 3 The Manifestation of Jesus at the Wedding of Cana

6. The Gospel of John is filled with signs that reveal the identity of Jesus. The first of these signs takes place at a wedding in Cana (John 2:1-11). What role does Mary play in this first sign?

7. What is revealed about Jesus in the changing of water into wine (John 2:11)? And what is the significance of a wedding setting?

8. What does Jesus mean when he says, "My hour has not yet come" (John 2:4)? (See John 7:30; 8:20; 12:23; 13:1; 17:1-5.)

Day 4 The Proclamation of the Kingdom of God

9. How do the following passages help you to understand Jesus' teaching about the kingdom of God? (See Matt 4:17; 6:10, 33; 12:28; 13:24-33; Mark 4:30-32; 10:13-16; Luke 9:57-62; 17:20-21; 22:27-30.)

10. In what ways does the life of Jesus make God's kingdom real to you? (See John 1:18; Col 1:15; 1 John 4:12.)

11. What are some examples of how God's kingdom has an impact on the world in which we live? Where is there evidence that God's kingdom is alive and well?

Day 5 The Transfiguration

12. Who is present at the Transfiguration of Jesus (Matt 17:1-8; Mark 9:2-13; Luke 9:28-36) and what might their presence mean?

13. In all three accounts a voice from the clouds identifies Jesus as the beloved or chosen Son and includes an admonition to "listen to him." Are you able to recognize both the divine and human elements in Jesus, and to listen carefully to his words?

14. The Transfiguration is often described as a glimpse of the glory to come. When have you experienced moments that are transforming and hopeful?

Day 6 The Institution of the Eucharist

15. Review the four accounts of the Lord's Supper (Mark 14:22-25; Matt 26:26-29; Luke 22:14-23; 1 Cor 11:23-26). Do you find any details in the various accounts that you had not noticed before?

16. The Gospels contain many accounts of Jesus sharing meals with his followers and others (for example, see Mark 6:34-44; 14:3-9; Luke 7:36; 10:38-42). Why do you suppose Jesus waited until the final hours of his life to identify himself with the food that was being shared?

17. Look at one of the versions of the multiplication of loaves and fish (Matt 14:13-21; 15:32-39; Mark 6:34-44; 8:1-9; Luke 9:10-17; John 6:1-14). How does this story foreshadow the Last Supper?

18. When Jesus identified himself with the bread and wine at the Last Supper, he ensured every generation of his presence in these tangible elements. In what ways has sharing in the body and blood of Christ equipped you to share the good news of his presence in our world?

Suggestion: Consider how each of these luminous mysteries sheds light on who Jesus is and who you are called to be.

LESSON 3

Touching the Mysteries: Scripture and the Rosary
Reflecting on the Mysteries of the Rosary, **pages 34–43**

The Sorrowful Mysteries

Day 1 The Agony in the Garden

1. Peter, James, and John were with Jesus when he was transfigured, and now go with him into the garden as he faces his agony (Matt 17:1; 26:36-37; Mark 9:2;14:32-33). How do you think these events shaped them and their understanding of what it means to follow Jesus?

2. Jesus prays in the garden, "Father, if you are willing, take this cup away from me; still, not my will but yours be done" (Luke 22:42).

   a) What is the "cup" to which Jesus refers? (See Matt 20:22; Mark 10:38-40; 14:23-24.)

   b) Because Jesus followed the will of God, he met with resistance and eventual death. When you pray for God's will in your life, what do you understand that to mean? (See John 6:37-40; 1 Tim 2:3-4; 2 Pet 3:9.) *accept what happens*

3. What can you learn about facing suffering in your life from the way that Jesus faced his own suffering?

Day 2 The Scourging at the Pillar

4. What is the purpose of the scourging of Jesus according to Matthew 27:26 and Mark 15:15? And how is the scourging presented with a different purpose in John 19:1-6?

5. The Gospel of Mark focuses on disciples following in the way of Jesus, the way of the cross (see Mark 8:34; 13:9-13). Do the disciples indeed experience some of what Jesus did? (See Acts 5:40-42; 16:22-24; 2 Cor 6:3-5; 11:24-25.)

6. In what ways does suffering in the name of Jesus continue to occur in our world?

Day 3 The Crowning with Thorns

7. Given the accusations against Jesus (Matt 27:11-12; Mark 15:2; John 18:33-37) and the way he preached about the kingdom of God (Matt 5:3-12; Mark 10:43-45; Luke 17:20-21), what does his crown come to symbolize?

8. What kind of kingdom did Jesus establish and embody? (See for example Matt 6:19-21; 18:1; Luke 12:22-34; John 13:34-35.)

9. What standards does our world use to measure success? How does your faith equip you to use a different standard of measurement?

    money & power

Day 4 Carrying the Cross

10. Simon of Cyrene was "pressed into service" to carry the cross of Jesus (Matt 27:32). How does this unknown figure become a model of discipleship? (See Matt 5:41.) *Be assertive*

11. Jesus instructs his followers to carry their crosses (Matt 10:38; Luke 14:27). How has your understanding of carrying your cross changed over the years? Does it get any easier?

12. In churches around the world, stations of the cross allow local communities to walk the way of the cross with Jesus. How can you make this spiritual practice an exercise in discipleship?

Day 5 The Crucifixion   *few of anger and sadness*

13. Read one of the following accounts of the crucifixion: Matt 27:33-56; Mark 15:22-41; Luke 23:33-49; John 19:17-30. What kind of emotional response does the account produce in you? How would you tell the story to others?

14. The commentary and footnotes for the various accounts describe the process of crucifixion in Roman times. Is there any part of that information that is new to you, or changes the way you understand what happened when Jesus was crucified?

15. How does Luke use both mockery (Luke 23:33-38) and confession (Luke 23:39-43) to demonstrate the meaning of Jesus' life and death?

Day 6

16. Paul says "the message of the cross is foolishness to those who are perishing, but to us who are being saved it is the power of God" (1 Cor 1:18). How was Jesus able to transform the meaning of the cross? (See Col 1:19-22; Rom 5:6-11; 6:6; 1 Pet 2:24.)

17. Both Mark (15:34) and Matthew (27:46) record a final soulful prayer of Jesus: "My God, my God, why have you forsaken me?"

    a) Can you relate to feeling that God has forsaken or forgotten you?

    b) Jesus' words are taken from Psalm 22. Read the psalm in its entirety and comment on what it teaches you about Jesus' final prayer.

18. Who are those who stay to witness the death of Jesus and what can they teach us? (See Matt 27:50-56; Mark 15:37-41; Luke 23:46-49; John 19:25-30.)

Suggestion: Consider the way in which your own sufferings and small acts of dying to self help you to relate to the suffering of Christ.

LESSON 4

Touching the Mysteries: Scripture and the Rosary
Reflecting on the Mysteries of the Rosary, **pages 46–55**

The Glorious Mysteries

Day 1 The Resurrection

1. a) Is the empty tomb itself proof of the Resurrection? (See Matt 27:62-66; John 20:1-10.)

   b) What proof is offered that Jesus is indeed raised from the dead? (See Mark 16:9-13; Matt 28:6-7; John 20:19-29; Acts 2:32; 3:15.)

2. How do Israel's sacred writings (Job 19:25-26; Ps 16:9-10; Isa 53:10-11; Hos 13:14) and the sayings of Jesus (Mark 9:9-10; John 2:18-22; 6:39) prepare his followers to recognize the Resurrection?

3. What promise does the Resurrection of Jesus hold for us? (See John 6:39-40; Rom 6:4; 8:11; 2 Cor 13:4; Phil 3:20-21.)

Day 2 The Ascension

4. What is the purpose of the Ascension of Christ according to Mark (16:19-20)? And according to Luke (24:36-53; Acts 1:1-12)?

5. Although John's Gospel does not record the Ascension itself, it does offer some teaching of Jesus that helps to make sense of the resurrection. What insights do you gain from John 16:1-33? (Also see John 14:12-31.)

6. In what ways has the Spirit within you given you the assurance you need to carry on the mission of Jesus in the world today?

Day 3 The Descent of the Holy Spirit

7. At Pentecost (Acts 2:1-4), the Spirit is physically manifest in wind and tongues of fire. How are these signs associated with other manifestations of God's presence? (For wind, see Gen 1:1-2; 8:1; Exod 10:13-14; for fire, see Exod 3:1-4; 13:21-22; 1 Kgs 18:36-39.)

8. How was the Pentecost event "repeated" in Caesarea (Acts 10:1-49)?

9. a) The fruit and gifts of the Spirit are signs of God's presence at work in each of us. Examine these lists and identify those areas where you see evidence of the Spirit in you. (See Gal 5:22-23; 1 Cor 12:4-11.)

   b) What is the purpose of such spiritual gifts? (See 1 Cor 12:12, 27-31; 13:1-3.)

Day 4 The Assumption

10. Paul refers to Jesus as the "firstfruits of those who have fallen asleep" (1 Cor 15:20). How is the church's teaching on the Assumption of Mary an extension of that teaching?

11. In what ways did Mary participate in the life and death of Jesus so as to experience his resurrection? (See John 19:25-27; 1 Pet 4:13.)

Day 5 Coronation of the Blessed Virgin Mary

12. In what ways does the belief in Mary's coronation as queen of heaven affirm the divinity of Jesus and the role Mary had as his mother?

13. In the book of Revelation, the woman surrounded by the sun, moon, and stars is understood as a symbol of God's people throughout salvation history (Rev 12:1-2). Why would this image be used to portray Mary as queen of heaven?

14. When praying the Hail Mary we say "pray for us now and at the hour of our death." Why is Mary seen as the consummate intercessor for us? What is the role of intercession in your own prayer life?

Suggestion: Consider the moments of glory or exultation that you have experienced as a way to recognize the glory that Christ promises to us.

Day 6 Summary

In Pope John Paul II's apostolic letter *The Rosary of the Virgin Mary,* he states: "The rosary, though clearly Marian in character, is at heart a Christ-centered prayer."

15. How has this study of twenty decades of the rosary helped you appreciate its emphasis on Christ?

16. Which of the mysteries gives you new insight for your own prayer life? Why?

17. Consider your own life as a reflection on the mystery of Christ. What kind of mystery is it? Joyful, Luminous, Sorrowful, Glorious? Some of each? Something else altogether?

NOTES